Introduction

Pick up your needles and knit some warmth for those you love!

This collection of **Hats, Mittens and Scarves** includes super styles for all! Edie Eckman has a definite talent for designing easy-to-wear knit accessories that are really fun to make. Create a whole wardrobe for yourself and gift sets for others. You'll come back to this collection time and time again, year after year—and you'll always find a design that will be perfect in a new yarn color to go with each new winter coat and jacket.

Many of the nine sets are sized for adults as well as children, so don't presume that if we've photographed them on children that they can't be made for a teen or adult.

Design Directory	page
Checked Out	30
Classy Cuffs	8
Dashing Dots	14
For the Slopes	21
Jolly Jester	11
Primary Colors	18
Rainbow Stripes	5
Reverse Stripes	24
Tie One On	26

General Directions

A Word about Our Sizes
Many of the patterns in this book include sizes for both children and adults. The child sizes are given in small, medium and large, with small being 2-4 years, medium 6-8 years and large 10-12 years.

A Word about the Yarns
These wonderful sets have been created using the following yarns: Coats & Clark Red Heart® Super Saver® and Classic® and Lion Brand® Yarns Wool-Ease®. Any yarns that achieve the specified gauges may be substituted.

An Important Word about Gauge
A correct stitch gauge is very important. Please take the time to work a stitch gauge swatch about 4" x 4". Measure the swatch. If the number of stitches and rows are fewer than indicated under "Gauge" in the pattern, your needles are too large. Try another swatch with smaller size needles. If the number of stitches and rows are more than indicated under "Gauge" in the pattern, your needles are too small. Try another swatch with larger size needles.

About Zeros
In patterns which include various sizes, zeros are sometimes necessary. For example, K0 (0, 1) means if you are making size Small or size Medium, you would do nothing and if you are making a size Large, you would K1.

Pompon Instructions
Cut two 1½"-diameter cardboard circles. Cut a hole in the center of each circle, about ½" in diameter. Thread a tapestry needle with 72" length of yarn, doubled. Then holding both circles together, insert needle through center hole, over outside edge, through center again **(Fig 1)** until entire circle is covered and center hole is filled **(thread more lengths of yarn as needed)**.

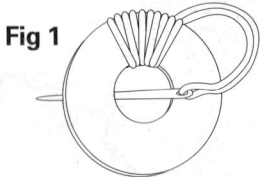

Fig 1

The pompons photographed in this book used 5 to 8 yds of yarn each.

With sharp scissors, cut yarn between the two circles all around the circumference **(Fig 2)**.

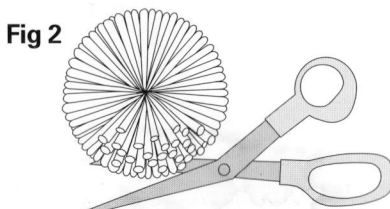

Fig 2

Using two 12" strands of yarn, slip yarn between circles and overlap yarn ends 2 or 3 times **(Fig 3)**—prevents tying knot from slipping, pull tightly and tie into a firm knot. Remove cardboards and fluff out pompon by rolling it between your hands. Trim evenly with scissors, leaving tying ends for attaching pompon to project.

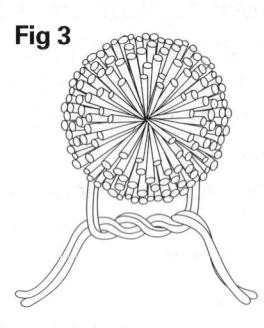

Fig 3

Fringe Instructions
Cut a piece of cardboard half as long as specified in instructions for strands plus ½" for trimming allowance. Wind yarn loosely and evenly lengthwise around cardboard. When card is filled, cut yarn across one end. Do this several times, then begin fringing; you can wind additional strands as you need them.

Single Knot Fringe
Hold specified number of strands for one knot of fringe together, then fold in half. Hold afghan with right side facing you. Use crochet hook to draw folded end through space or stitch from right to wrong side **(Figs 4 and 5)**, pull loose ends through folded section **(Fig 6)** and draw knot up firmly **(Fig 7)**. Space knots as indicated in pattern instructions.

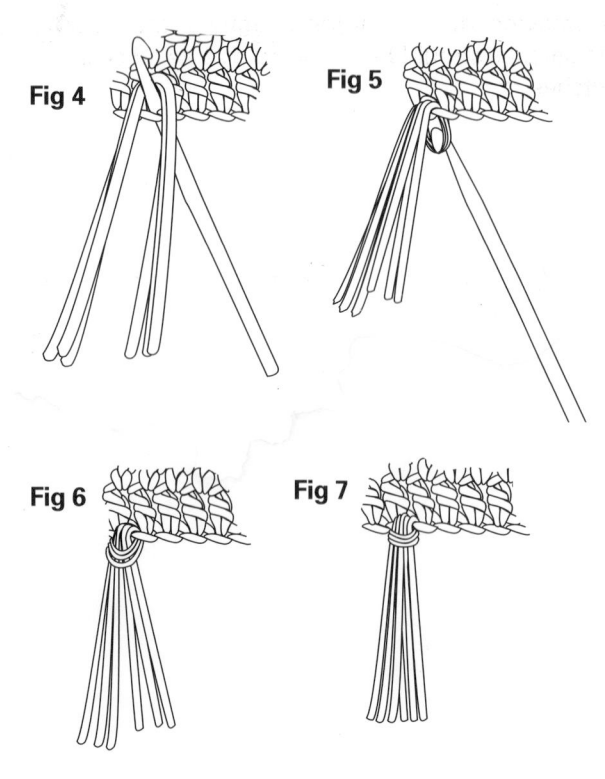

Fig 4 Fig 5

Fig 6 Fig 7

Special Technique

Weaving On Two Needles—Kitchener Stitch

Thread yarn into tapestry needle; with wrong sides together, work from right to left as follows:

Step 1:
Insert tapestry needle into first stitch on front needle as to purl **(Fig 1)**. Draw yarn through stitch, leaving stitch on knitting needle.

Step 2:
Insert tapestry needle into first stitch on back needle as to purl **(Fig 2)**. Draw yarn through stitch and slip stitch off knitting needle.

Step 3:
Insert tapestry needle into next stitch on same **(back)** needle as to knit **(Fig 3)**, leaving stitch on knitting needle.

Step 4:
Insert tapestry needle into first stitch on front needle as to knit **(Fig 4)**. Draw yarn through stitch and slip stitch off knitting needle.

Step 5:
Insert tapestry needle into next stitch on same **(front)** needle as to purl **(Fig 5)**. Draw yarn through stitch, leaving stitch on knitting needle.

Repeat Steps 2 through 5 until one stitch is left on each needle. Then repeat Steps 2 through 4. Finish off.

Hint:
When weaving, do not pull yarn tightly or too loosely; woven stitches should be the same size as adjacent knitted stitches.

Fig 1
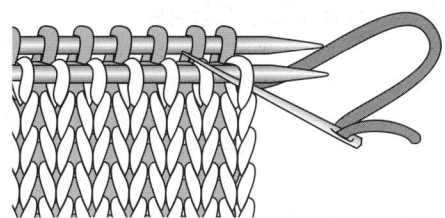

Fig 2
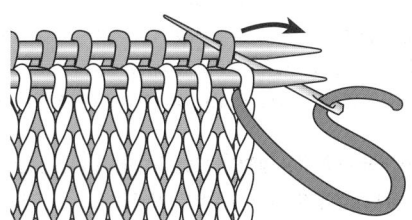

Fig 3
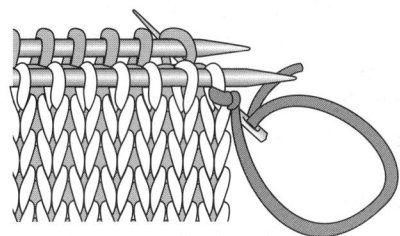

Fig 4
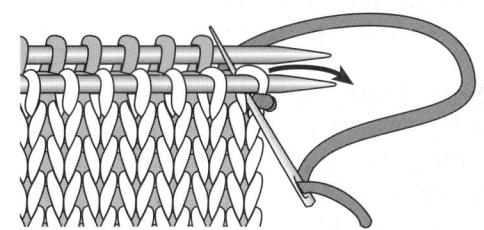

Fig 5
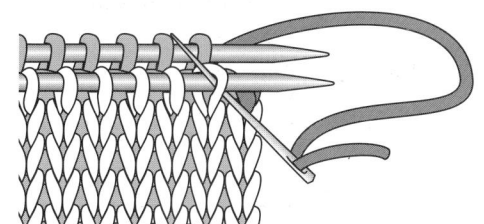

Abbreviations and Symbols

beg	begin(ning)
dec	decrease
gm(s)	gram(s)
inc	increase
K	knit
K2 tog	knit 2 together
oz	ounce(s)
P	purl
P2 tog	purl 2 together
patt	pattern
prev	previous
PSSO	pass slipped stitch over
P2SSO	pass 2 slipped stitches over
rem	remain(ing)
rep	repeat(ing)
rnd(s)	round(s)
sl	slip
sl st(s)	slip stitch(es)
SSK	slip, slip, knit
st(s)	stitch(es)
tbl	through back loop
tog	together
yb	yarn back
yd	yard(s)
yf	yarn front

* An asterisk (or double asterisk **) is used to mark the beginning of a portion of instructions to be worked more than once; thus, "rep from * twice more" means after working the instructions once, repeat the instructions following the asterisk twice more (3 times in all).

— The number after a long dash at the end of a row or round indicates the number of stitches you should have when the row or round has been completed.

() Parentheses are used to enclose instructions which should be worked the exact number of times specified immediately following the parentheses, such as "(K2, P2) twice."

[ ] Brackets and parentheses () are also used to provide additional information to clarify instructions.

Rainbow Stripes

Sizes:
Hat and Mittens: Child small (child medium, child large, adult)
Scarf: Child (adult)

Finished Measurements:
Hat: 19" (20", 21", 22") circumference
Mittens: 5" (6", 6½", 7½") long with cuff
Scarf: 8" x 45" (9" x 58")
Note: Hat and Mitten instructions are written for size child small; changes for larger sizes are in parentheses. Scarf instructions are written for size child; changes for size adult are in parentheses.

Materials:

For Hat:
Worsted weight yarn, 1 (1, 1½, 1½) oz [70 (70, 105, 105) yds, 35 (35, 52, 52) gms] blue; 10 yds each, red, yellow, orange, and green

For Mittens:
Worsted weight yarn, 1 (1, 1½, 1½) oz [70 (70, 105, 105) yds, 35 (35, 52, 52) gms] blue; 10 yds each, red, yellow, orange, and green

For Scarf:
Worsted weight yarn, 7 (8) oz [490 (560) yds, 245 (280) gms] blue; 10 yds each, red, yellow, orange, and green
Note: Our models were made with Red Heart® Classic™, Olympic Blue #849, Cherry Red #912, Yellow #230, and Tangerine #253; Red Heart® Super Saver®, Grass Green #687
Size 8 (5mm) straight knitting needles, or size required for gauge (for hat and scarf)
Size 6 (4.25mm) straight knitting needles (for hat and scarf)
Size 8 (5mm) double-pointed knitting needles, or size required for gauge (for mittens)
Size 6 (4.25mm) double-pointed knitting needles (for mittens)
Stitch markers
Stitch holder (for mittens)
Size 16 tapestry needle
Crochet hook (for attaching tassels)

Gauge:
With larger size needles:
20 sts and 24 rows = 4" in stockinette st

Instructions

Hat

Border:
With smaller size straight needles and blue, cast on 80 (84, 88, 92) sts.

Row 1 (right side):
Knit.

Row 2:
Knit. Cut blue.

Rows 3 and 4:
With red, knit. Cut red.

Rows 5 and 6:
With yellow, knit. Cut yellow.

Rows 7 and 8:
With green, knit. Cut green.

Rows 9 and 10:
With orange, knit. Cut orange.

Body:
Change to larger size needles.

Row 1:
With blue, * K19 (20, 21, 22), inc (knit in front and back of next st); rep from * 3 times more—84 (88, 92, 96) sts.

Row 2:
Purl.

Row 3:
Knit.

Rep Rows 2 and 3 until body measures 5" (5½", 6", 7") from beg, ending by working a Row 2.

Shaping:
Row 1:
K18 (19, 20, 21), K2 tog; * K19 (20, 21, 22), K2 tog; rep from * twice more; K1—80 (84, 88, 92) sts.

Row 2:
Purl.

Row 3:
Knit.

continued

Rainbow Stripes (continued)

Row 4:
P17 (18, 19, 20), P2 tog; * P18 (19, 20, 21), P2 tog; rep from * twice more; P1—76 (80, 84, 88) sts.

Row 5:
Knit.

Row 6:
Purl.

Row 7:
K16 (17, 18, 19) sts, K2 tog; * K17 (18, 19, 20), K2 tog; rep from * twice more; K1—72 (76, 80, 84) sts.

Rows 8 and 9:
Rep Rows 2 and 3.

Row 10:
P15 (16, 17, 18), P2 tog; * P16 (17, 18, 19), P2 tog; rep from * twice more; P1—68 (72, 76, 80) sts.

Rows 11 and 12:
Rep Rows 5 and 6.

Row 13:
K14 (15, 16, 17), K2 tog; * K15 (16, 17, 18), K2 tog; rep from * twice more; K1—64 (68, 72, 76) sts.

Rows 14 and 15:
Rep Rows 2 and 3.

Row 16:
P13 (14, 15, 16), P2 tog; * P14 (15, 16, 17), P2 tog; rep from * twice more; P1—60 (64, 68, 72) sts.

Rows 17 and 18:
Rep Rows 5 and 6.

Row 19:
K12 (13, 14, 15), K2 tog; * K13 (14, 15, 16), K2 tog; rep from * twice more; K1—56 (60, 64, 68) sts.

Rows 20 and 21:
Rep Rows 2 and 3.

Row 22:
P11 (12, 13, 14), P2 tog; * P12 (13, 14, 15), P2 tog; rep from * twice more; P1—52 (56, 60, 64) sts.

Continue working in stockinette st, dec every 3rd row in same manner until 6 sts rem.

Cut yarn, leaving a 24" end. Draw yarn through rem sts and pull tight.

Finishing:
Step 1:
Hold piece with wrong side facing you and side edges together. With tapestry needle and long end, and carefully matching colors, sew seam.

Step 2:
Cut two 8" lengths each of red, yellow, green, and orange. Hold strands together and fold in half. Use crochet hook to draw folded end through peak of hat. Pull loose ends through folded section and draw knot up firmly. Trim ends even.

Mitten (make 2)
With smaller size double-pointed needles and blue, cast on 24 (28, 32, 36) sts. Divide evenly on 3 needles; join, being careful not to twist sts. Mark beg of rnds.

Cuff:
Rnd 1:
Purl.

Rnd 2:
Knit.

Rnd 3:
Purl. Cut blue.

Rnds 4 and 5:
With red, rep Rnds 2 and 3. Cut red.

Rnds 6 and 7:
With yellow, rep Rnds 2 and 3. Cut yellow

Rnds 8 and 9:
With green, rep Rnds 2 and 3. Cut green.

Rnds 10 and 11:
With orange, rep Rnds 2 and 3. Cut orange.

Palm:
Rnd 1:
With blue, K6 (8, 10, 12), inc (knit in front and back of next st); K10, inc; K6 (8, 10, 12)—26 (30, 34, 38) sts.

Rnds 2 through 4 (5, 6, 7):
Knit.

Thumb Gusset:
Note: Slip markers as you come to them.

Rnd 1:
Inc twice; place marker; K24 (28, 32, 36)—28 (32, 36, 40) sts.

Rnd 2:
Knit.

Rnd 3:
Inc; K2, inc; K24 (28, 32, 36)—30 (34, 38, 42) sts.

Rnd 4:
Knit.

Rnd 5:
Inc; K4, inc; K24 (28, 32, 36)—32 (36, 40, 44) sts.

Rnd 6:
Knit.

Rnd 7:
Inc; K6, inc; K24 (28, 32, 36)—34 (38, 42, 46) sts.

Rnd 8:
Knit.

For Size Child Small Only:
Continue with Dividing Rnd on page 7.

For Sizes Child Medium, Child Large, and Adult Only:
Rnd 9:
Inc; K8, inc; K28 (32, 36)—40 (44, 48) sts.

Rnd 10:
Knit.

For Sizes Child Medium and Child Large, continue with Dividing Rnd below.

For Size Adult Only:
Rnd 11:
Inc; K10, inc; K36—52 sts.

Rnd 12:
Knit.

Dividing Rnd (all sizes):
K10 (12, 12, 14), remove marker; place these sts on stitch holder; K24 (28, 32, 36).

Knit every rnd until mitten measures 4 1/2" (5 1/2", 6", 7") from cuff.

Shape Top:
Rnd 1:
* K2, K2 tog; rep from * 5 (6, 7, 8) times more—18 (21, 24, 27) sts.

Rnd 2:
Knit.

Rnd 3:
* K1, K2 tog; rep from * 5 (6, 7, 8) times more—12 (14, 16, 18) sts.

Rnd 4:
Knit.

Rnd 5:
* K2 tog; rep from * 5 (6, 7, 8) times more.

Cut yarn, leaving a 7" end. Draw end through rem sts and pull tight.

Thumb:
Divide 10 (12, 12, 14) sts from stitch holder onto 3 larger size double-pointed needles; with blue, pick up one st in thumb joining—11 (13, 13, 15) sts.

Rnd 1:
K9 (11, 11, 13), K2 tog.

Rnd 2:
Knit.

Rep Rnd 2 until thumb measures 1" (1 1/4", 1 1/2", 2") from thumb joining.

Next Rnd:
* K2 tog; rep from * 4 (5, 5, 6) times more.

Cut yarn, leaving a 7" end. Draw end through rem sts and pull tight. Weave in all ends.

Scarf
With smaller size straight needles and blue, cast on 34 (40) sts.

Row 1 (right side):
Knit.

Rows 2 and 3:
Knit. Cut blue.

Rows 4 and 5:
With red, knit. Cut red.

Rows 6 and 7:
With yellow, knit. Cut yellow.

Rows 8 and 9:
With green, knit. Cut green.

Rows 10 and 11:
With orange, knit. Cut orange.

Change to larger size needles.

Row 12:
With blue, knit.

Row 13:
K5, P24 (30), K5.

Rows 14 through 17:
Rep Rows 12 and 13 twice more.

Note: The next two rows create extra length on the sides of the scarf so that the garter stitch edges do not pull up and distort the scarf.

Row 18:
K5, turn; K5, turn; K34 (40).

Row 19:
K5, turn; K5, turn; K5, P24 (30), K5.

Rep Rows 12 through 19 in sequence until scarf measures 40" (53").

Change to smaller size needles.

Ending Rows:
Rows 1 through 8:
Rep Rows 4 through 11.

With blue, knit three rows.

Bind off.

Weave in all ends.

Classy Cuffs

Size:
Adult

Finished Measurements:
Hat: 22" circumference
Mittens: 7½" long with cuff
Scarf: 10" x 58"

Materials:

For Hat:
Worsted weight yarn, 2 oz (140 yds, 57 gms) off white; 1 oz (70 yds, 28 gms) grey

For Mittens:
Worsted weight yarn, 2 oz (140 yds, 57 gms) off white; 1 oz (70 yds, 28 gms) grey

For Scarf:
Worsted weight yarn, 8 oz (560 yds, 224 gms) off white; 2 oz (140 yds, 57 gms) grey

Note: Our models were made with Lion Brand® Wool-Ease®, Fisherman #99 and Oxford Grey #152

Size 8 (5mm) double-pointed knitting needles, or size required for gauge (for hat and mittens)
Size 8 (5mm) 24" circular needle, or size required for gauge (for hat)
Size 8 (5mm) straight knitting needles, or size required for gauge (for scarf)
Stitch markers
Small stitch holder (for mittens)
Size 16 tapestry needle

Gauge:
20 sts and 24 rows = 4" in patt st

Special Abbreviation

Slip, Slip, Knit (SSK):
Slip next 2 sts, one at a time, as to knit; insert left-hand needle through both sts from right to left; K2 tog—SSK made.

Instructions

Hat

Cuff:
With circular needle and grey, cast on 105 sts; join, being careful not to twist sts.

Mark beg of rnds.

Rnd 1 (right side):
Knit.

Rnd 2:
K2 tog; (K1, YO, K1) in next st; * sl 1 as to knit, K2 tog; PSSO; (K1, YO, K1) in next st; rep from * 24 times more; SSK (see Special Abbreviation).

Rnd 3:
With off white, knit.

Rnd 4:
Rep Rnd 2.

Rnds 5 through 16:
Rep Rnds 1 through 4 three times more. At end of Rnd 16, cut grey.

Rnd 17:
With off white, knit. Turn, and flip work over needle so wrong side of work becomes right side.

Ribbing:

Rnd 1 (right side):
* K8, K2 tog; rep from * 8 times more; K6—96 sts.

Rnd 2:
* K1, P1; rep from * around.

Rep Row 2 until ribbing measures 2", inc one st by knitting in front and back of last st on last rnd—97 sts.

Continuing with off white, rep Rnds 1 and 2 of cuff until hat measures 5" from ribbing, ending by working a Rnd 1.

Crown:

Note: When necessary, change to double-pointed needles.

Rnd 1:
K2 tog; * K1, sl 1 as to knit, K2 tog; PSSO; rep from * 22 times more; K1, SSK—51 sts.

Rnd 2:
Knit.

Rnd 3:
K2 tog; * SSK; rep from * 23 times more; K1—26 sts.

Rnd 4:
Knit.

Rnd 5:
* SSK; rep from * 12 times more—13 sts.

Cut yarn, leaving a 7" end. Draw end through rem sts and pull tight. Weave in all ends.

Finishing:
Step 1:
Turn up cuff.

Step 2 (optional):
With grey, make 3" pompon following instructions on page 2.

Mitten (make 2)
With double-pointed needles and grey, cast on 41 sts; join, being careful not to twist sts.

Mark beg of rnds.

Cuff:
Rnd 1 (right side):
With grey, knit.

Rnd 2:
K2 tog; * (K1, YO, K1) in next st; sl 1 as to knit, K2 tog, PSSO; rep from * 8 times more; (K1, YO, K1) in next st; SSK (see Special Abbreviation on page 8).

Rnd 3:
With off white, knit.

Rnd 4:
Rep Rnd 2.

Rnds 5 through 16:
Rep Rnds 1 through 4 three times more. At end of Rnd 16, cut grey.

Rnd 17:
With off white, knit.
Turn and flip work around needle so wrong side of work becomes right side.

Rnd 18:
* K6, K2 tog; rep from * 4 times more; K1—36 sts.

Ribbing:
Rnd 1:
(K1, P1) 18 times.
Rep Rnd 1 until ribbing measures 2¼".

Next Rnd:
K1, P1, inc (knit in front and back of next st); P1, (K1, P1) 16 times—37 sts.

Body:
Rnds 1 through 6:
With off white, rep Rnds 1 and 2 of cuff three times.

Rnd 7:
Knit.

Thumb Gusset:
Note: Slip markers as you come to them.
Rnd 1:
K2 tog; * (K1, YO, K1) in next st; sl 1 as to knit, K2 tog, PSSO; rep from * twice more; (K1, YO, K1) in next st; sl 1 as to knit, K1, PSSO; place marker; inc twice; place marker; K1, K2 tog; ** (K1, YO, K1) in next st; sl 1 as to knit, K2 tog, PSSO; rep from ** twice more; (K1, YO, K1) in next st; SSK—39 sts.

Rnd 2:
Knit.

Rnd 3:
K2 tog; * (K1, YO, K1) in next st; sl 1 as to knit, K2 tog, PSSO; rep from * twice more; (K1, YO, K1) in next st; sl 1 as to knit, K1, PSSO; slip marker; inc; K2, inc; slip marker; K1, K2 tog; ** (K1, YO, K1) in next st; sl 1 as to knit, K2 tog, PSSO; rep from ** twice more; (K1, YO, K1) in next st; SSK—41 sts.

Rnd 4:
Knit.

Rnd 5:
K2 tog; * (K1, YO, K1) in next st; sl 1 as to knit, K2 tog, PSSO; rep from * twice more; (K1, YO, K1) in next st; sl 1 as to knit, K1, PSSO; slip marker; inc; K4, inc; slip marker; K1, K2 tog; ** (K1, YO, K1) in next st; sl 1 as to knit, K2 tog, PSSO; rep from ** twice more; (K1, YO, K1) in next st; SSK—43 sts.

Rnd 6:
Knit.

Rnd 7:
K2 tog; * (K1, YO, K1) in next st; sl 1 as to knit, K2 tog, PSSO; rep from * twice more; (K1, YO, K1) in next st; sl 1 as to knit, K1, PSSO; slip marker; inc; K6, inc; slip marker; K1, K2 tog; ** (K1, YO, K1) in next st; sl 1 as to knit, K2 tog, PSSO; rep from ** twice more; (K1, YO, K1) in next st; SSK—45 sts.

Rnd 8:
Knit.

Rnd 9:
K2 tog; * (K1, YO, K1) in next st; sl 1 as to knit, K2 tog, PSSO; rep from * twice more; (K1, YO, K1) in next st; sl 1 as to knit, K1, PSSO; slip marker; inc; K8, inc; slip marker; K1, K2 tog; ** (K1, YO, K1) in next st; sl 1 as to knit, K2 tog, PSSO; rep from ** twice more; (K1, YO, K1) in next st; SSK—47 sts.

Rnd 10:
Knit.

continued

Classy Cuffs (continued)

Rnd 11:
K2 tog; * (K1, YO, K1) in next st; sl 1 as to knit, K2 tog, PSSO; rep from * twice more; (K1, YO, K1) in next st; sl 1 as to knit, K1, PSSO; slip marker; inc; K10, inc; slip marker; K1, K2 tog; ** (K1, YO, K1) in next st; sl 1 as to knit, K2 tog, PSSO; rep from ** twice more; (K1, YO, K1) in next st; SSK—49 sts.

Divide for Thumb:
Rnd 1:
Knit to second marker; place last 14 sts worked onto stitch holder; remove one marker; knit rem sts.

Rnd 2:
K2 tog; * (K1, YO, K1) in next st; sl 1 as to knit, K2 tog, PSSO; rep from * twice more; (K1, YO, K1) in next st; SSK; slip marker; sl 1, K2 tog, PSSO; ** (K1, YO, K1) in next st; sl 1 as to knit, K2 tog, PSSO; rep from ** twice more; (K1, YO, K1) in next st; SSK—34 sts.

Rnd 3:
Knit.

Rnd 4:
K2 tog; * (K1, YO, K1) in next st; sl 1 as to knit, K2 tog, PSSO; rep from * twice more; (K1, YO, K1) in next st; sl 2 as to knit, remove marker, K2 tog, P2SSO; ** (K1, YO, K1) in next st; sl 1 as to knit, K2 tog, PSSO; rep from ** twice more; (K1, YO, K1) in next st; SSK—33 sts.

Rnd 5:
Knit.

Rnd 6:
K2 tog; * (K1, YO, K1) in next st, sl 1, K2 tog, PSSO; rep from * 6 times more; (K1, YO, K1) in next st; SSK.

Rnd 7:
Knit.

Rep Rnds 6 and 7 until mitten measures 7" or desired length from ribbing, ending by working a knit row.

Shape Top:
Rnd 1:
K2 tog; (K1, sl 1 as to knit, K2 tog, PSSO) 7 times; K1, SSK—17 sts.

Rnd 2:
Knit.

Rnd 3:
K2 tog; SSK 7 times; K1—9 sts.

Cut yarn, draw end through rem sts and pull tight. Weave in all ends.

Thumb:
Divide 14 sts from stitch holder onto 3 double-pointed needles; with off white, pick up one st at thumb joining—15 sts.

Rnd 1:
K13, K2 tog—14 sts.

Rnd 2:
Knit.

Rep Rnd 2 until thumb measures 2" from thumb joining.

Next Rnd:
K2 tog seven times.

Cut yarn, draw end through rem sts and pull tight. Weave in all ends.

Scarf

Section (make 2):
With straight needles and grey, cast on 49 sts.

Row 1 (wrong side):
Purl.

Row 2 (right side):
K2 tog; * (K1, YO, K1) in next st; sl 1 as to knit, K2 tog, PSSO; rep from * 10 times more; (K1, YO, K1) in next st; SSK (see Special Abbreviation on page 8).

Row 3:
With off white, purl.

Row 4:
Rep Row 2.

Rep Rows 1 through 4 until piece measures 5" from cast-on edge.

Rep Rows 3 and 4 until piece measures 29".

Bind off loosely.

Hold sections with right sides together and bound-off edges at top. With tapestry needle and carefully matching sts, sew together.

Jolly Jester

Sizes:
Hat and Mittens: Child small (medium)
Scarf: One size

Finished Measurements:
Hat: 19" (20") circumference
Mittens: 7" long with ribbing
Scarf: 7" x 45"
Note: Hat and mitten instructions are written for size small; changes for size medium are in parentheses.

Materials:
For Hat (both sizes):
Worsted weight yarn, 1 oz (70 yds, 30 gms) each, gold, purple, and teal

For Mittens (both sizes):
Worsted weight yarn, 1 oz (70 yds, 30 gms) each, gold, purple, and teal

For Scarf:
Worsted weight yarn, 5 oz (350 yds, 150 gms) each, gold, purple, and teal
Note: Our models were made with Red Heart® Super Saver®, Teal #388, Amethyst #356, and Gold #321
Size 8 (5mm) straight knitting needles, or size required for gauge (for hat and scarf)
Size 8 (5mm) double-pointed knitting needles, or size required for gauge (for mittens)
Size 6 (4.25mm) double-pointed knitting needles (for mittens)
Stitch markers
Large stitch holder (for hat)
Small stitch holder (for mittens)
2 large bobbins (for scarf)
Size 16 tapestry needle
Crochet hook (for attaching tassels)

Gauge:
16 sts and 28 rows = 4" in patt st

Instructions

Hat
Ribbing:
With larger size straight needles and teal, cast on 85 (89) sts.

Row 1 (right side):
K1; * P1, K1; rep from * across.

Row 2:
P1; * K1, P1; rep from * across.

Rep Rows 1 and 2 until ribbing measures 2" from cast-on edge, ending by working a wrong side row. Cut teal.

Gold Body:
Foundation Row (right side):
Join gold; K7 (8); * K2 tog; K5; rep from * 3 times more; K2 tog; K6 (7)—38 (40) sts.

Place unworked 42 (44) sts onto stitch holder.

Row 1 (wrong side):
* K2, P2; rep from * 8 (9) times more; K2 (0).

Row 2 (right side):
P2 (0); * K2, P2; rep from * 8 (9) times more.

Row 3:
* P2, K2; rep from * 8 (9) times more; P2 (0).

Row 4:
K2 (0); * P2, K2; rep from * 8 (9) times more.

Rep Rows 1 through 4 until piece measures 3" (4") from ribbing, ending by working a Row 4. Mark each side.

Peaks:
FOR SIZE SMALL ONLY:
Row 1:
K2 tog; P2; * K2, P2; rep from * to last 2 sts; K2 tog—36 sts.

Row 2:
P1; * K2, P2; rep from * to last 3 sts; K2, P1.

Row 3:
K2 tog; K1; * P2, K2; rep from * to last 5 sts; P2, K1, K2 tog—34 sts.

Row 4:
* P2, K2; rep from * to last 2 sts; P2.

Row 5:
P2 tog; K2; * P2, K2; rep from * to last 2 sts; P2 tog—32 sts.

continued

11

Jolly Jester (continued)

Row 6:
K1; * P2, K2; rep from * to last 3 sts; P2, K1.

Row 7:
P2 tog; P1; * K2, P2; rep from * to last 5 sts; K2, P1, P2 tog—30 sts.

Row 8:
* K2, P2; rep from * to last 2 sts; K2.

Rows 9 through 32:
Rep Rows 1 through 8 three times more. At end of Row 32—6 sts.
Cut yarn, leaving a 24" end. Draw end through rem sts and pull tight.

FOR SIZE MEDIUM ONLY:

Row 1:
K2 tog; * P2, K2; rep from * to last 2 sts; P2 tog—38 sts.

Row 2:
K1; * P2, K2; rep from * to last st; P1.

Row 3:
K2 tog; K1; * P2, K2; rep from * to last 3 sts; P1, P2 tog—36 sts.

Row 4:
K2; * P2, K2; rep from * to last 2 sts; P2.

Row 5:
P2 tog; * K2, P2; rep from * to last 2 sts; K2 tog—34 sts.

Row 6:
P1; * K2, P2; rep from * to last st; K1.

Row 7:
P2 tog; P1; * K2, P2; rep from * to last 3 sts; K1, K2 tog—32 sts.

Row 8:
* P2, K2; rep from * across.

Rows 9 through 32:
Rep Rows 1 through 8 three times more.

Rows 33 and 34:
Rep Rows 1 and 2. At end of Row 34—6 sts.
Cut yarn, leaving a 24" end. Draw end through rem sts and pull tight.

Purple Body and Peaks:
Place 42 (**44 sts**) from stitch holder onto straight needle; join purple.

Foundation Row (right side):
K7 (**8**); * K2 tog; K5; rep from * 3 times more; K7 (**8**)—38 (**40**) sts.
Work same as for Gold Body beginning with Row 1 of body on page 11.

Finishing

Step 1:
With 24" gold end at peak, weave gold edges together to marker. Sew one gold edge only to corresponding purple edge from markers to ribbing.

Step 2:
With 24" purple end at peak, weave purple edges together to marker. Sew one purple edge only to corresponding gold edge from markers to ribbing. Sew ribbing seam.

Tassel (make 2)
Cut ten 8" strands of teal. For each tassel, hold 5 strands together and fold in half. Use crochet hook to draw folded end through one peak of hat. Pull loose ends through folded section and draw knot up firmly. Repeat with remaining strands in second peak. Trim ends even.

Mitten (make 2)

Ribbing:
With smaller size double-pointed needles and teal, cast on 26 sts. Divide onto 3 needles. Join, being careful not to twist sts.

Rnd 1:
* K1, P1; rep from * around.

Rep Rnd 1 until ribbing measures 2½" from beg.

Body (make one gold and one purple):
Join gold or purple; cut teal. Change to larger size double-pointed needles.

Rnd 1:
Knit.

Rnd 2:
K1, K2 tog; (P2, K2) twice; P2, K1, K2 tog; (P2, K2) twice; P2—24 sts.

Rnd 3:
* K2, P2; rep from * around.

Rnd 4:
* P2, K2; rep from * around.

Rnd 5:
Rep Rnd 4.

Rnds 6 and 7:
Rep Rnd 3.

FOR SIZE SMALL ONLY:
Continue with Thumb Gusset below.

FOR SIZE MEDIUM ONLY:

Rnds 8 through 11:
Rep Rnds 4 through 7 once more.

Thumb Gusset (both sizes):

Rnd 1:
P2; place marker; inc (knit in front and back of next st); inc in next st; place marker; (P2, K2) 5 times—26 sts.

Note: Slip markers as you come to them.

Rnd 2:
P2, K4, (P2, K2) 5 times.

Rnd 3:
K2, inc; K2, inc; (K2, P2) 5 times—28 sts.

Rnd 4:
K10, P2, (K2, P2) 4 times.

Rnd 5:
P2, inc; K4, inc; (P2, K2) 5 times—30 sts.

Rnd 6:
P2, K8, (P2, K2) 5 times.

Rnd 7:
K2, inc; K6, inc; (K2, P2) 5 times—32 sts.

Rnd 8:
K14, P2, (K2, P2) 4 times.

For Size Small, gusset is complete. Continue with Palm below.

Rnd 9:
P2, inc; K8, inc; (P2, K2) 5 times—34 sts.

Rnd 10:
P2, K12, (P2, K2) 5 times.

For Size Medium, gusset is complete.

Palm:
FOR SIZE SMALL ONLY:
Dividing Rnd:
P2; sl next 10 sts onto stitch holder; (P2, K2) 5 times—22 sts.

Rnd 1:
K2, (K2, P2) 5 times.

Rnd 2:
P2, (P2, K2) 5 times.

Rnd 3:
Rep Rnd 2.

Rnd 4:
Rep Rnd 1.

Rep Rnds 1 through 4 until mitten measures 4$\frac{1}{2}$" from top of ribbing, ending on any rnd.
Continue with top shaping below.

FOR SIZE MEDIUM ONLY:
Dividing Rnd:
K2; sl next 12 sts onto stitch holder; (K2, P2) 5 times—22 sts.

Rnd 1:
K2, (K2, P2) 5 times.

Rnd 2:
P2, (P2, K2) 5 times.

Rnd 3:
Rep Rnd 2.

Rnd 4:
Rep Rnd 1.

Rep Rnds 1 through 4 until mitten measures 4$\frac{3}{4}$" from top of ribbing, ending on any rnd.

Top Shaping (both sizes):
Rnd 1:
K1, (K2 tog, K1) 7 times—15 sts.

Rnd 2:
Knit.

Rnd 3:
K1, (K2 tog) 7 times—8 sts.

Cut yarn, leaving a 7" end. Draw end through rem sts and pull tight.

Thumb:
Divide 10 (12) sts from stitch holder onto 3 needles; join matching color.

Rnd 1:
Pick up one st at thumb joining; K9 (11), K2 tog—10 (12) sts.

Rnd 2:
Knit.

Rep Rnd 2 until thumb measures 1" (1$\frac{1}{2}$") from thumb joining.

Next Rnd:
(K2 tog) 5 (6) times.

Cut yarn, draw end through rem sts and pull tight. Weave in all ends.

Scarf
Note: Wind one bobbin with teal, and one bobbin with purple. When changing color on following rows, bring new color under old color to prevent holes in work. Always change colors on wrong side of work. Join new colors as needed.

With larger size straight needles and teal, cast on 28 sts.

Row 1 (right side):
* K2, P2; rep from * across.

Row 2:
Rep Row 1.

Row 3:
* P2, K2; rep from * across.

Row 4:
Rep Row 3.

Rows 5 through 12:
Rep Rows 1 through 4 twice more.

Row 13:
With teal, (K2, P2) twice; with purple, K12; with teal, (K2, P2) twice.

Row 14:
With teal, (K2, P2) twice; with purple, (K2, P2) 3 times; with teal, (K2, P2) twice.

Row 15:
With teal, (P2, K2) twice; with purple, (P2, K2) 3 times; with teal, (P2, K2) twice.

Row 16:
Rep Row 15.

Rows 17 and 18:
Rep Row 14.

continued

Jolly Jester (continued)

Rows 19 and 20:
Rep Row 15.

Row 21:
With teal, (K2, P2) twice; with purple, K2, P2; with gold, K4; with purple, K2, P2; with teal, (K2, P2) twice.

Row 22:
With teal, (K2, P2) twice; with purple, K2, P2; with gold, K2, P2; with purple, K2, P2; with teal, (K2, P2) twice.

Row 23:
With teal, (P2, K2) twice; with purple, P2, K2; with gold, P2, K2; with purple, P2, K2; with teal, (P2, K2) twice.

Row 24:
Rep Row 23.

Rows 25 and 26:
Rep Row 22.

Rep Rows 23 through 26 until piece measures about 42" from beg, ending by working a Row 26. Cut gold.

Ending Section:
Row 1:
With teal, (P2, K2) twice; with purple, P2, K6, P2, K2; with teal, (P2, K2) twice.

Cut unused strand of purple.

Row 2:
With teal, (P2, K2) twice; with purple, (P2, K2) 3 times; with teal, (P2, K2) twice.

Row 3:
With teal, (K2, P2) twice; with purple, (K2, P2) 3 times; with teal, (K2, P2) twice.

Row 4:
Rep Row 3.

Rows 5 and 6:
Rep Row 2.

Rows 7 and 8:
Rep Row 3.

At end of Row 8, cut purple and unused strand of teal.

Row 9:
With teal, (P2, K2) twice; K12, (P2, K2) twice.

Row 10:
(P2, K2) 14 times.

Row 11:
(K2, P2) 14 times.

Row 12:
Rep Row 11.

Rows 13 and 14:
Rep Row 10.

Rows 15 through 18:
Rep Rows 11 through 14.

Rows 19 and 20:
Rep Rows 11 and 12.

Bind off in patt.

Dashing Dots

Sizes:
Hat and Mittens: Child medium (child large, adult)
Scarf: Child (adult)

Finished Measurements:
Hat: 20" (21", 22") circumference
Mittens: 6" (6½", 7½") long with cuff
Scarf: 8" x 48" (9½" x 58")

Note: Hat and mitten instructions are written for size child medium; changes for larger sizes are in parentheses. Scarf instructions are written for size child; changes for size adult are in parentheses.

Materials:

For Hat:
Worsted weight yarn, 5½ (6, 6) oz [360 (395, 395) yds; 154 (170, 170) gms] each, off white and purple; 3 (3, 3) oz, [197 (197, 197) yds, 85 (85, 85) gms] grey

For Mittens:
Worsted weight yarn, 1 (2, 2) oz [70 (105, 105) yds, 35 (35, 35) gms] each, off white and purple; ½ (½, ½) oz [35 (35, 35) yds, 27 (27, 27) gms] grey

For Scarf:
Worsted weight yarn, 8 (10) oz [560 (700) yds, 280 (350) gms] each, off white and purple; ½ (½) oz [35 (35) yds, 27 (27) gms] grey

Note: Our models were made with Lion Brand® Wool-Ease®, Grape Heather #144, Grey Heather #151, and Fisherman #099

Size 8 (5mm) straight knitting needles, or size required for gauge (for scarf)
Size 8 (5mm) 16" circular knitting needle, or size required for gauge (for mittens)
Size 8 (5mm) double-pointed knitting needles, or size required for gauge (for mittens)
Size 6 (4.25mm) 16" circular knitting needle (for hat)

Size 6 (4.25mm) double-pointed knitting needles
   (for mittens)
Stitch markers
Stitch holder (for mittens)
Size 16 tapestry needle

Gauge:
On larger size needles:
19 sts and 38 rows = 4" in patt

Slip Stitch Pattern I (for hat and mittens):
Rnds 1 and 2:
Knit.

Rnd 3:
* Sl 1 as to purl, K1; rep from * around.

Rnd 4:
* Yb, sl 1 as to purl, yf, P1; rep from * around.

Rnds 5 and 6:
Knit.

Rnd 7:
* K1, sl 1 as to purl; rep from * around.

Rnd 8:
* Yf, P1, yb, sl 1 as to purl, P1; rep from * around..

Instructions

Hat

Border:
With smaller size circular needle and purple, cast on 86 (90, 94) sts. Join, being careful not to twist sts.

Rnd 1:
Knit.

Rnd 2:
Purl.

Rnds 3 through 6:
Rep Rnds 1 and 2 twice more.
Change to larger size circular needle. Unless otherwise specified, carry unused colors along side edge.

Body:
Rnds 1 and 2:
With purple, work Rnds 1 and 2 of Slip Stitch Pattern I.

Rnds 3 and 4:
With grey, work Rnds 3 and 4 of Slip Stitch Pattern I.

Rnds 5 and 6:
With off white, work Rnds 5 and 6 of Slip Stitch Pattern I.

Rnds 7 and 8:
With purple, work Rnds 7 and 8 of Slip Stitch Pattern I.

Rnds 9 and 10:
With grey, work Rnds 1 and 2 of Slip Stitch Pattern I.

Rnds 11 and 12:
With off white, work Rnds 3 and 4 of Slip Stitch Pattern I. Cut grey and off white.

Rnds 13, 15, and 17:
With purple, knit.

Rnds 14, 16, and 18:
With purple, purl.

Rnds 19 and 20:
With purple, work Rnds 1 and 2 of Slip Stitch Pattern I.

Rnds 21 and 22:
With off white, work Rnds 3 and 4 of Slip Stitch Pattern I.

Rnds 23 and 24:
With purple, work Rnds 5 and 6 of Slip Stitch Pattern I.

Rnds 25 and 26:
With off white, work Rnds 7 and 8 of Slip Stitch Pattern I.

Rep Rnds 19 through 26 until hat measures 6½" (6½", 7") from beg. Cut off white.

Shape Crown:
Note: Change to larger size double-pointed needles as necessary.

Rnd 1:
With purple, K1; * K2, K2 tog; rep from * to last st; K1— 65 (68, 71) sts.

Rnd 2:
Knit.

Rnd 3:
* K1, K2 tog; rep from * to last 2 sts; K2 tog.

Rnds 4 and 5:
* K2 tog; rep from * around.

Cut yarn, leaving a 7" end. Draw end through rem sts and pull tight. Weave in all ends.

Following instructions on page 2, make 3" pompon with equal number of strands of each color.

Mitten (make 2)
With purple and smaller size double-pointed needles, cast on 28 (32, 38) sts. Join, being careful not to twist sts. Mark beg of rnds.

Rnd 1:
Knit.

Rnd 2:
Purl.

Rnds 3 through 6:
Rep Rnds 1 and 2 twice more.

Change to larger size double-pointed needles. Unless otherwise specified, carry unused colors along side edge.

continued

Dashing Dots (continued)

Cuff:

Rnds 1 and 2:
With purple, work Rnds 1 and 2 of Slip Stitch Pattern I on page 15.

Rnds 3 and 4:
With grey, work Rnds 3 and 4 of Slip Stitch Pattern I.

Rnds 5 and 6:
With off white, work Rnds 5 and 6 of Slip Stitch Pattern I.

Rnds 7 and 8:
With purple, work Rnds 7 and 8 of Slip Stitch Pattern I.

Rnds 9 and 10:
With grey, work Rnds 1 and 2 of Slip Stitch Pattern I.

Rnds 11 and 12:
With off white, work Rnds 3 and 4 of Slip Stitch Pattern I. Cut grey and off white.

Rnds 13, 15, and 17:
With purple, knit.

Rnds 14, 16, and 18:
With purple, purl.

Rnds 19 and 20:
With purple, work Rnds 1 and 2 of Slip Stitch Pattern I.

Rnds 21 and 22:
With off white, work Rnds 3 and 4 of Slip Stitch Pattern I.

FOR SIZE CHILD MEDIUM ONLY:
Continue with Thumb Gusset below.

FOR SIZES CHILD LARGE AND ADULT ONLY:

Rnds 23 and 24:
With purple, rep Rnds 5 and 6 of Slip Stitch Pattern I.

Rnds 25 and 26:
With off white, work Rnds 7 and 8 of Slip Stitch Pattern I. Continue with Thumb Gusset.

Thumb Gusset:

Note: Slip markers as you come to them.

Rnd 1:
With purple, K13 (15, 18); place marker, K2; place marker, K13 (15, 18).

Rnd 2:
With purple, K13 (15, 18); inc (knit in front and back of next st) twice; K13 (15, 18)—30 (34, 40) sts.

Rnd 3:
With off white, work in Slip Stitch Pattern I as established to first marker; K4; continue in Slip Stitch Pattern I.

Rnd 4:
With off white, work in patt as established to first marker; inc; K2, inc; continue in patt—32 (36, 42) sts.

Rnd 5:
With purple, work in patt to first marker; K6; continue in patt.

Rnd 6:
With purple, work in patt to first marker; inc; K4, inc; continue in patt—34 (38, 44) sts.

Rnd 7:
With off white, work in patt to first marker; K8; continue in patt.

Rnd 8:
With off white, work in patt to first marker; inc; K6, inc; continue in patt—36 (40, 46) sts.

Rnd 9:
With purple, work in patt to first marker; K10; continue in patt.

Rnd 10:
With purple, work in patt to first marker; inc; K8, inc; continue in patt—38 (42, 48) sts.

FOR SIZE CHILD MEDIUM ONLY:
Continue with Divide for Thumb below.

FOR SIZES CHILD LARGE AND ADULT ONLY:

Rnd 11:
With off white, work in patt to first marker; K12; continue in patt.

Rnd 12:
With off white, work in patt to first marker; inc; K10, inc; continue in patt—44 (50) sts.

Continue with Divide for Thumb.

Divide for Thumb:

Rnd 1:
Work in patt to first marker; K12 (12, 14); slip these sts onto stitch holder; remove markers; continue in patt.

Rnd 2:
Work in patt around.

Rep Rnd 2 until mitten measures 6" (6$\frac{1}{2}$", 6$\frac{3}{4}$") from first grey row, ending by working a Rnd 4 or a Rnd 8 of patt. Cut off white.

Shape Top:

Rnd 1:
With purple, knit.

Rnd 2:
Purl.

Rnd 3:
* K2, K2 tog; rep from * 5 (7, 7) times more; K2 (0, 2)—20 (24, 26) sts.

Rnd 4:
Purl.

Rnd 5:
* K1, K2 tog; rep from * 5 (7, 7) times more; K2 (0, 2)—14 (16, 18) sts.

Rnd 6:
Purl.

Rnd 7:
* K2 tog; rep from * around—7 (8, 9) sts. Cut yarn, leaving a 7" end. Draw end through rem sts and pull tight. Weave in all ends.

Thumb:
Divide 12 **(12, 14)** sts on stitch holder onto 3 double-pointed needles; pick up one st at thumb joining.

Rnd 1:
With off white, K11 **(11, 13)**, K2 tog—12 **(12, 14)** sts.

Rnd 2:
Knit.

Rnds 3 and 4:
With purple, knit.

Rnds 5 and 6:
With off white, knit.

Rep Rnds 3 through 6 until thumb measures $1\frac{1}{4}$" **($1\frac{1}{2}$", 2")** from thumb joining, changing colors every two rows.

Next Rnd:
* K2 tog; rep from * around.
Cut yarn, leaving a 7" end. Draw end through rem sts and pull tight. Weave in all ends.

Slip Stitch Pattern II (for scarf):
Row 1:
Knit.

Row 2:
K2; purl to last 2 sts; K2.

Row 3:
K3; * sl 1 as to purl, K1; rep from * to last 2 sts; K2.

Row 4:
K3; * yf, sl 1 as to purl, yb, K1; rep from * to last 2 sts; K2.

Row 5:
Knit.

Row 6:
K2; purl to last 2 sts; K2.

Row 7:
K4; * sl 1 as to purl, K1; rep from * to last 3 sts; K3.

Row 8:
K4; * yf, sl 1 as to purl, yb, K1; rep from * to last 3 sts; K3.

Scarf
Note: Carry unused yarn along edge, twisting every other row.

Edging:
With purple and straight needles, cast on 37 **(45)** sts.

Rows 1 through 6:
Knit.

Body:
Rows 1 and 2:
With purple, work Rows 1 and 2 of Slip Stitch Pattern II above.

Rows 3 and 4:
With grey, work Rows 3 and 4 of Slip Stitch Pattern II.

Rows 5 and 6:
With off white, work Rows 5 and 6 of Slip Stitch Pattern II.

Rows 7 and 8:
With purple, work Rows 7 and 8 of Slip Stitch Pattern II.

Rows 9 and 10:
With grey, rep Rows 1 and 2 of Slip Stitch Pattern II.

Rows 11 and 12:
With off white, rep Rows 3 and 4 of Slip Stitch Pattern II.

Rows 13 and 14:
With purple, rep Rows 5 and 6 of Slip Stitch Pattern II.

Rows 15 and 16:
With grey, rep Rows 7 and 8 of Slip Stitch Pattern II.

Rows 17 and 18:
With off white, rep Rows 1 and 2 of Slip Stitch Pattern II.

Rows 19 and 20:
With purple, rep Rows 3 and 4 of Slip Stitch Pattern II.

Rows 21 and 22:
With grey, rep Rows 5 and 6 of Slip Stitch Pattern II.

Rows 23 and 24:
With off white, rep Rows 7 and 8 of Slip Stitch Pattern II.

Rows 25 through 30:
With purple, knit.

Rows 31 and 32:
With purple, rep Rows 1 and 2 of Slip Stitch Pattern II.

Rows 33 and 34:
With off white, rep Rows 3 and 4 of Slip Stitch Pattern II.

Rows 35 and 36:
With purple, rep Rows 5 and 6 of Slip Stitch Pattern II.

Rows 37 and 38:
With off white, rep Rows 7 and 8 of Slip Stitch Pattern II.

Rep Rows 31 through 38 until scarf measures about 44" **(54")**, ending by working a Row 36.

Next Six Rows:
With purple, knit.

Ending Border:
Rows 1 through 24:
Rep Rows 1 through 24 of body.

Edging:
With purple, knit 6 rows.
Bind off.

17

Primary Colors

Sizes:
Hat and Mittens: Child small (medium)
Scarf: One size

Finished Measurements:
Hat: 19" (20") circumference
Mittens: 5" (6") long
Scarf: 7½" x 45" without colored ends
Note: Hat and mitten instructions are written for size small; changes for larger size are in parentheses.

Materials:

For Hat (both sizes):
Worsted weight yarn, 1 oz (70 yds, 28 gms) black; 20 yds each, red, yellow, orange, green, and blue

For Mittens (both sizes):
Worsted weight yarn, 1 oz (70 yds, 28 gms) black; 20 yds each, red, yellow, orange, green, and blue

For Scarf:
Worsted weight yarn, 6 oz (420 yds, 170 gms) black; 20 yds each, red, yellow, orange, green, and blue

Note: Our models were made with Red Heart Super Saver®, Black #312, Hot Red #390, Bright Yellow #324, Vibrant Orange #354, Grass Green #687, and Skipper Blue #384

Size 8 (5mm) straight knitting needles, or size required for gauge (for hat and scarf)
Size 8 (5mm) double-pointed knitting needles, or size required for gauge (for mittens)
8 large yarn bobbins
Stitch markers
Stitch holder (for mittens)
Size 16 tapestry needle

Gauge:
16 sts and 32 rows = 4" in garter st (knit every row)

Triangle Pattern:
With designated color and straight needles, cast on 2 sts.

Row 1:
Inc (knit in front and back of next st); K1.

Row 2:
Inc; K2.

Row 3:
Inc; knit rem sts.
Rep Row 3 until number of sts indicated are on needle.
Knit two rows, leaving sts on needle. Do not cut yarn.

Instructions

Note: Wind 8 bobbins as follows: 2 red, 2 yellow, 2 green, 1 orange, 1 blue.

Hat

Cuff:
With straight needles and wound bobbins, make 8 triangles with 10 sts each on same needle following Triangle Pattern in following color sequence: yellow, green, orange, red, blue, yellow, green, red.

Note: Triangles should have bobbins on right-hand side of triangle. When changing colors on Row 1 below, bring new color under old color to prevent holes in work.

Row 1 (right side):
With red, K10; with green, K10; with yellow, K10; with blue, K10; with red, K10; with orange, K10; with green, K10; with yellow, K10—80 sts.

Row 2:
With yellow, K10; bring yellow to front, twist with green, bring green to back, K10; bring green to front, twist with orange, bring orange to back, K10; bring orange to front, twist with red, bring red to back, K10; bring red to front, twist with blue, bring blue to back, K10; bring blue to front, twist with yellow, bring yellow to back, K10; bring yellow to front, twist with green, bring green to back, K10; bring green to front, twist with red, bring red to back, K10; bring red to front.

Rows 3 through 6:
Rep Rows 1 and 2 twice more. At end of Row 6, join black; cut all other colors.

Rows 7 and 8:
Knit.

Row 9 (turning ridge):
Purl.

Body:
Row 1 (right side**):**
Knit.

Rep Row 1 until black section measures 5" (6") from beg.

Crown:
Row 1:
* K6, K2 tog; rep from * 9 times more—70 sts.

Row 2:
Knit.

Row 3:
* K5, K2 tog; rep from * 9 times more—60 sts.

Row 4:
Knit.

Row 5:
* K4, K2 tog; rep from * 9 times more—50 sts.

Row 6:
Knit.

Row 7:
* K3, K2 tog; rep from * 9 times more—40 sts.

Row 8:
Knit.

Row 9:
* K2, K2 tog; rep from * 9 times more—30 sts.

Row 10:
Knit.

Row 11:
* K1, K2 tog; rep from * 9 times more—20 sts.

Row 12:
Knit.

Row 13:
K2 tog 10 times—10 sts.

Row 14:
Knit.

Cut yarn, leaving a 24" end for sewing. Draw end through rem sts and pull tight.

Tassels
With black, cast on 9 sts, leaving a 7" end for sewing.

Rows 1 and 2:
Knit.

Row 3:
With orange, K3, leaving rem sts unworked.

Rep Row 3 until orange section measures 2" from beg. Bind off.

Join green in next unused st on Row 2.

Rep Row 3 until green section measures 2" from beg. Bind off.

Join blue in next unused st on Row 2.

Rep Row 3 until blue section measures 2" from beg. Bind off.

Finishing
Step 1:
With long end and tapestry needle, sew seam. Sew black base of tassels to top of hat, shaping base into a circle.

Step 2:
Weave in all ends.

Step 3:
Turn up cuff along turning ridge; sew seam loosely along third ridge of triangles.

Mitten (make 2**)**
Note: Wind 6 bobbins as follows: 1 each orange, blue, and yellow for one mitten; 1 each red, green, and orange for 2nd mitten.

Cuff:
With straight needles and wound bobbins, make 3 triangles with 9 sts each following Triangle Pattern. Make triangles in one of the following color sequences: orange, blue, and yellow; or red, green, and orange.

Note: Triangles should have bobbins on right-hand side of triangle. When changing colors on Row 1 below, bring new color under old color to prevent holes in work.

Row 1 (right side**):**
With first color, K9; with 2nd color, K9; with 3rd color, K9—27 sts.

Row 2:
With first color, K9; bring first color to front, twist with 2nd color, bring 2nd color to back, K9; bring 2nd color to front, twist with third color, bring third to back, K9; bring 3rd color to front.

Rows 3 through 6:
Rep Rows 1 and 2 twice more. At end of Row 6, join black; cut all colors.

Note: Remainder of mitten is worked in rnds. Divide sts evenly on 3 double-pointed needles. Mark beg of rnds.

Rnd 1:
Knit.

FOR SIZE SMALL ONLY:
Rnd 2:
P1, P2 tog; P24—26 sts. Continue with Rnd 3 on page 20.

continued

Primary Colors (continued)

FOR SIZE MEDIUM ONLY:

Rnd 2:
* P1, inc (purl in front and back of st); P6; rep from * twice more—30 sts.

Rnd 3 (turning ridge both sizes):
Turn work so wrong side is facing you by pushing cuff through center of needles; working in opposite direction, knit.

Rnd 4:
Purl.

Rnd 5:
Knit.

Rep Rnds 4 and 5 until black section measures 1½" (1¾") from beg, ending by working a purl rnd.

Thumb Gusset:

Note: To inc for gusset, knit in front and back of next st.

Rnd 1:
K12 (14); place marker; inc twice; place marker; K12 (14)—28 (32) sts.

Rnd 2:
Purl.

Rnd 3:
K12 (14), inc; K2, inc; K12 (14)—30 (34) sts.

Rnd 4:
Purl.

Rnd 5:
K12 (14), inc; K4, inc; K12 (14)—32 (36) sts.

Rnd 6:
Purl.

Rnd 7:
K12 (14), inc; K6, inc; K12 (14)—34 (38) sts.

Rnd 8:
Purl.

FOR SIZE SMALL ONLY:
Continue with Divide For Thumb below.

FOR SIZE MEDIUM ONLY:

Rnd 9:
K14, inc; K8, inc; K14—40 sts.

Rnd 10:
Purl.

Divide for Thumb (both sizes):

Rnd 1:
K22 (24), place last 10 (12) sts worked onto stitch holder; remove markers; K12 (14)—24 (28) sts.

Rnd 2:
Purl.

Rnd 3:
Knit.

Rnd 4:
Purl.

Rep Rnds 3 and 4 until black section measures 5" (5½") from beg or desired length, ending with a purl row.

Shape Top:

Rnd 1:
* K2, K2 tog; rep from * 5 (6) times more—18 (21) sts.

Rnd 2:
Purl.

Rnd 3:
* K1, K2 tog; rep from * 5 (6) times more—12 (14) sts.

Rnd 4:
Purl.

Rnd 5:
K2 tog 6 (7) times—6 (7) sts.

Cut yarn, draw end through rem sts and pull tight. Weave in all ends.

Thumb:
Divide 10 (12) sts from stitch holder onto 3 double-pointed needles; join black.

Rnd 1:
Pick up one st at thumb joining; P9 (11), P2 tog—10 (12) sts.

Rnd 2:
Knit.

Rnd 3:
Purl.

Rep Rnds 2 and 3 until thumb measures 1" (1¼") from inside of thumb joining, ending with a purl rnd.

Next Rnd:
K2 tog 5 (6) times.

Cut yarn, draw end through rem sts and pull tight.

Tack points to mitten. Weave in ends.

Scarf

Note: Wind 6 bobbins as follows: one yellow, one green, 2 red, one orange, and one blue.

With straight needles and wound bobbins, make 3 triangles on same needle with 10 sts each, following Triangle Pattern on page 18, in following color sequence: one yellow; one green; one red.

Triangles should have bobbins on right-hand side of triangle. When changing colors on Row 1 below, bring new color under old color to prevent holes in work.

Row 1 (right side):
With red, K10; with green, K10; with yellow, K10—30 sts.

Row 2:
With yellow, K10; bring yellow to front, twist with green, bring green to back, K10; bring green to front, twist with red, bring red to back, K10; bring red to front.

Rows 3 through 6:
Rep Rows 1 and 2 twice more. At end of Row 6, join black; cut all colors.

Row 7:
Knit.

Rep Row 7 until black section of scarf measures 45" long, ending on a wrong side row. Cut black.

Ending Triangles:
Row 1:
Join orange, K10; join blue, K10; join red, K10—30 sts.

Row 2:
With red, K10; bring red to front, twist with blue, bring blue to back, K10; bring blue to front, twist with orange, bring orange to back, K10; bring orange to front.

Rows 3 through 6:
Rep Rows 1 and 2 twice more.

Do not twist colors on following rows.

Row 7:
With orange, K2 tog; K8; with blue, K2 tog; K8; with red, K2 tog; K8—27 sts.

Row 8:
With red, K2 tog; K7; with blue, K2 tog; K7; with orange, K2 tog; K7—24 sts.

Row 9:
With orange, K2 tog; K6; with blue, K2 tog; K6; with red, K2 tog; K6—21 sts.

Row 10:
With red, K2 tog; K5; with blue, K2 tog; K5; with orange, K2 tog; K5—18 sts.

Row 11:
With orange, K2 tog; K4; with blue, K2 tog; K4; with red, K2 tog; K4—15 sts.

Row 12:
With red, K2 tog; K3; with blue, K2 tog; K3; with orange, K2 tog; K3—12 sts.

Row 13:
With orange, K2 tog; K2; with blue, K2 tog; K2; with red, K2 tog; K2—9 sts.

Row 14:
With red, K2 tog; K1; with blue, K2 tog; K1; with orange, K2 tog; K1—6 sts.

Bind off each color separately.

For the Slopes

Size:
Hat and Mittens: Child medium (child large, adult)
Scarf: Child (adult)

Finished Measurements:
Hat: 20" (21", 22") circumference
Mittens: 6" ($6\frac{1}{2}$", $7\frac{1}{2}$") long with cuff
Scarf: 8" x 40" (9" x 57")
Note: Hat and mitten instructions are written for size child medium; changes for larger sizes are in parentheses. Scarf instructions are written for size child; changes for size adult are in parentheses.

Materials:
For Hat:
Worsted weight yarn, 1 ($1\frac{1}{2}$, $1\frac{1}{2}$) oz [70 (105, 105) yds, 28 (42, 42) gms] teal; $\frac{1}{2}$ (1, 1) oz [35 (70, 70) yds, 14 (28, 28) gms] blue

For Mittens:
Worsted weight yarn, 1 ($1\frac{1}{2}$, $1\frac{1}{2}$) oz [70 (105, 105) yds, 28 (42, 42) gms] each, blue, teal, and lime

For Scarf:
Worsted weight yarn, 5 (6) oz [350 (420) yds, 140 (154) gms] blue; 1 (1) oz [70 (70) yds, 28 (28) gms] each, lime and teal
Note: Our models were made with Red Heart Super Saver®, Skipper Blue #384, Kiwi #651, and Mint #366
Size 8 (5mm) straight knitting needles, or size required for gauge (for hat and scarf)
Size 7 (4.5mm) straight knitting needles (for hat)
Size 8 (5mm) double-pointed knitting needles, or size required for gauge (for mittens)
Stitch markers
Stitch holder (for mittens)
Size 16 tapestry needle
Crochet hook (for fringe)

Gauge:
With larger size needles:
16 sts and 24 rows = 4" in stockinette st

continued

For the Slopes (continued)

Special Abbreviation

Slip, Slip, Knit (SSK):
Slip next 2 sts, one at a time, as to knit; insert left-hand needle through both sts from right to left; K2 tog—SSK made.

Instructions

Hat

Brim:
With green and larger size straight needles, loosely cast on 80 (84, 88) sts.

Row 1 (wrong side):
Knit.

Row 2 (right side):
Purl.

Rows 3 through 12 (14, 16):
Rep Rows 1 and 2, 5 (6, 7) times more.

Row 13 (15, 17):
Knit.

Turning Ridge Row 14 (16, 18):
Knit.

Row 15 (17, 19):
Knit.

Row 16 (18, 20):
Purl.

Rows 17 (19, 21) through 26 (30, 34):
Rep Rows 15 (17, 19) and 16 (18, 20), 5 (6, 7) times more.

Hem Row (wrong side):
Turn brim at turning ridge, bringing cast-on row up to working row; * knit tog one st from needle and one st from cast-on row; rep from * across.

Next Row (right side):
Purl.

Change to blue and smaller size needles.

BODY:

Row 1 (wrong side):
Purl.

Row 2 (right side):
Knit.

Rep Rows 1 and 2 until hat measures 9" (10", 11") from turning row, ending by working a right side row.

Bind off.

Finishing

Hold hat with right sides together; with tapestry needle and corresponding colors, sew back seam. Sew seam across top edge. Do not cut yarn. Turn right side out and bring needle through seam to right side; bring top seam ends A and B together to form peaks (see diagrams); tack peaks together. Weave in yarn end on wrong side.

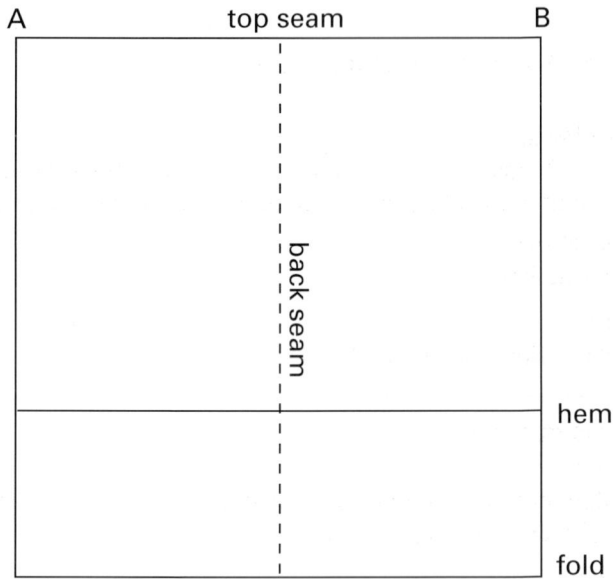

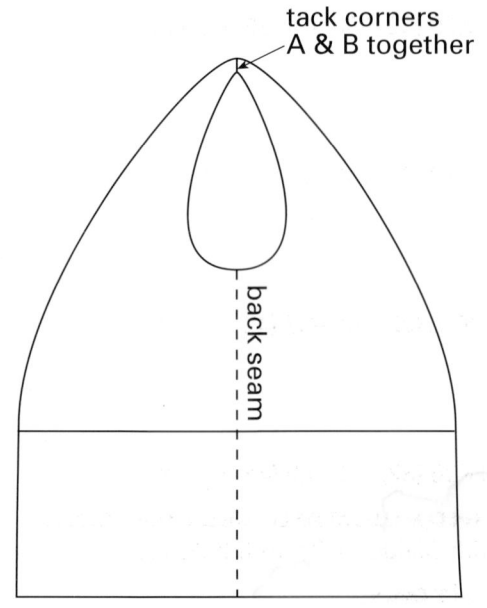

Mitten (make 2, one blue cuff and green body; one lime cuff and blue body)

CUFF:
With blue or green and double-pointed needles, loosely cast on 30 (34, 38) sts. Divide onto 3 needles. Join, being careful not to twist sts.

Rnds 1 through 9 (9, 10):
Knit.

Turning Rnd 10 (10, 11):
Purl.

Rnds 11 (11, 12) through 19 (19, 21):
Knit.

Hem Rnd:
Turn cuff inside along turning rnd; * knit tog one st from needle and one st from cast-on edge; rep from * around.

Next Rnd:
Purl. Cut first color.

BODY:

Rnds 1 through 10 (12, 12):
With second color, knit.

THUMB GUSSET:

Rnd 1:
Inc (knit in front and back of next st) twice; place marker; K28 (32, 36)—32 (36, 40) sts.

Rnd 2:
Knit.

Rnd 3:
Inc; K2, inc; K28 (32, 36)—34 (38, 42) sts.

Rnd 4:
Knit.

Rnd 5:
Inc; K4, inc; K28 (32, 36)—36 (40, 44) sts.

Rnd 6:
Knit.

Rnd 7:
Inc; K6, inc; K28 (32, 36)—38 (42, 46) sts.

Rnd 8:
Knit.

Rnd 9:
Inc; K8, inc; K28 (32, 36)—40 (44, 48) sts.

FOR SIZES CHILD MEDIUM AND CHILD LARGE ONLY:
Continue with Divide for Thumb below.

FOR SIZE ADULT ONLY:
Rnd 10:
Inc; K10, inc; K36—50 sts.

DIVIDE FOR THUMB (ALL SIZES):
Rnd 1:
K12 (12, 14), place last 12 (12, 14) sts worked onto stitch holder; remove marker; K28 (32, 36).

Rnd 2:
Knit.

Rep Rnd 2 until mitten measures 6$\frac{3}{4}$" (7$\frac{3}{4}$", 8$\frac{1}{2}$") from hem rnd.

SHAPE TOP:
Rnd 1:
* K2, K2 tog; rep from * around—21 (24, 27) sts.

Rnd 2:
Knit.

Rnd 3:
* K1, K2 tog; rep from * around—14 (16, 18) sts.

Rnd 4:
Knit.

Rnd 5:
K2 tog 7 (8, 9) times.

Cut yarn, draw end through rem sts and pull tight. Weave in all ends.

THUMB:
Divide 12 (12, 14) sts from stitch holder onto 3 needles; join matching color, pick up one st at thumb joining—13 (13, 15) sts.

Rnd 1:
K11 (11, 13), K2 tog—12 (12, 14) sts.

Rnd 2:
Knit.

Rep Rnd 2 until thumb measures 1$\frac{1}{4}$" (1$\frac{1}{2}$", 2") from thumb joining.

Next Rnd:
K2 tog 6 (6, 7) times.

Cut yarn, draw end through rem sts and pull tight. Weave in all ends.

Scarf

With straight needles and green, cast on 32 (36) sts.

Work garter st (knit every row) in following color sequence:

16 (24) rows green. Cut green.

12 (16) rows lime. Cut lime.

Work with blue for about 34" (48"). Cut blue.

12 (16) rows lime. Cut lime.

16 (24) rows green.

Knit one row.

Bind off.

Fringe

Following Fringe instructions on page 2, make Single Knot Fringe. Cut 8" strands, 2 each of blue, green, and lime; for each knot. Tie 5 (6) knots evenly spaced across each short end of scarf. Trim ends even.

Reverse Stripes

Size:
Hat and Mittens: Child small (child medium, child large, adult)
Scarf: Child (adult)

Finished Measurements:
Hat: 19" (20", 21", 22") circumference
Mittens: 5" (6", 6½", 7½") long with cuff
Scarf: 8" x 45" (10" x 58")
Note: Hat instructions are written for size child small; changes for larger sizes are in parentheses. Scarf instructions are written for size child; changes for size adult are in parentheses.

Materials:
For Hat:
Worsted weight yarn, 1 (1, 1½, 1½) oz [70 (70, 105, 105) yds, 35 (35, 52, 52) gms] each, blue and off white

For Mittens:
Worsted weight yarn, 1 (1, 1½, 1½) oz [70 (70, 105, 105) yds, 35 (35, 52, 52) gms] each, blue and off white

For Scarf:
Worsted weight yarn, 4 (5) oz [280 (350) yds, 120 (150) gms] each, blue and off white
Note: Our models were made with Lion Brand® Wool-Ease®, Blue Heather #107 and Fisherman #99
Size 8 (5mm) straight knitting needles, or size required for gauge (for scarf)
Size 8 (5mm) 16" circular knitting needle, or size required for gauge (for hat)
Size 8 (5mm) double-pointed knitting needles, or size required for gauge (for hat and mittens)
Size 6 (4.25mm) double-pointed knitting needles (for mittens)
Stitch markers
Stitch holder (for mittens)

Gauge:
With larger size needles:
20 sts and 24 rows = 4" in stockinette st

Instructions
Hat
Note: Unless otherwise specified, carry unused colors along side edge.
With circular needle and blue, cast on 84 (88, 92, 96) sts. Join, being careful not to twist yarn. Mark beg of rnds.

Rnds 1 through 6:
Knit. Cut blue.

Rnd 7:
With off white, knit.

Rnd 8:
* K1, P1; rep from * around.
Rep Rnd 8 until ribbing measures 1½" (2", 2", 2") from beg.

BODY:
Rnd 1:
Purl.

Rnds 2 and 3:
With blue, purl.

Rnds 4 and 5:
With off white, purl.
Rep Rows 2 through 5 until body measures 4" (4", 4½", 5") from top of ribbing, ending by working a Rnd 2 or 4.

CROWN:
Note: Change to larger size double-pointed needles and continue in stripe patt as established.

Rnd 1:
* P2; P2 tog; rep from * around—63 (66, 69, 72) sts.

Rnds 2 through 4:
Purl.

Rnd 5:
* P1, P2 tog; rep from * around—42 (44, 46, 48) sts.

Rnds 6 through 8:
Purl.

Rnd 9:
* P2 tog; rep from * around—21 (22, 23, 24) sts.

Rnd 10:
Purl.

Rnd 11:
* P2 tog; rep from * 9 (10, 10, 11) times more; P1 (0, 1, 0)—11 (11, 12, 12) sts.
Cut yarn, leaving a 7" end. Draw end through rem sts and pull tight. Weave in all ends.

Mitten (make 2)
With smaller size double-pointed needles and blue, cast on 26 (30, 34, 38) sts. Divide evenly on 3 needles. Join, being careful not to twist sts. Mark beg of rnds.

24

Cuff:
Rnds 1 through 5 (6, 6, 6):
Knit. Cut blue.
RIBBING:
Rnd 1:
With off white, knit.
Rnd 2:
* K1, P1; rep from * around.
Rep Rnd 2 until ribbing measures 2" (2", 2 1/2", 2 1/2").
Change to larger size double-pointed needles.

Palm:
Rnd 1:
Purl.
Note: Carry unused yarn loosely in back of work. Remainder of mitten is worked in following stripe pattern:
2 rnds blue
2 rnds off white
Rnds 2 through 5 (5, 7, 8):
Purl.

Thumb Gusset:
Note: Slip markers as you come to them.
Rnd 1:
P12 (14, 16, 18), place marker; inc (purl in front and back of next st) twice; place marker; P12 (14, 16, 18)—28 (32, 36, 40) sts.
Rnd 2:
Purl.
Rnd 3:
P12 (14, 16, 18), inc; P2, inc; P12 (14, 16, 18)—30 (34, 38, 42) sts.
Rnd 4:
Purl.
Rnd 5:
P12 (14, 16, 18), inc; P4, inc; P12 (14, 16, 18)—32 (36, 40, 44) sts.
Rnd 6:
Purl.
Rnd 7:
P12 (14, 16, 18), inc; P6, inc; P12 (14, 16, 18)—34 (38, 42, 46) sts.
Rnd 8:
Purl.
FOR SIZE CHILD SMALL ONLY:
Continue with Dividing Rnd.
FOR SIZES CHILD MEDIUM, LARGE, AND ADULT ONLY:
Rnd 9:
Inc; P14 (16, 18), inc; P8, inc; P14 (16, 18)—40 (44, 48).
Rnd 10:
Purl.

For Sizes Child Medium and Child Large, continue with Dividing Rnd below.
FOR SIZE ADULT ONLY:
Rnd 11:
P18, inc; P10, inc; P18—50 sts.
Rnd 12:
Purl.
Dividing Rnd (all sizes):
P22 (26, 28, 32); remove markers; place last 10 (12, 12, 14) sts worked onto stitch holder; P12 (14, 16, 18)—24 (28, 32, 36) sts.
Continuing to work in stripe pattern, purl every rnd until piece measures 4 1/2" (5 1/2", 6", 6 1/2") from ribbing.

Shape Top:
Rnd 1:
* P2, P2 tog; rep from * 5 (6, 7, 8) times more—18 (21, 24, 27) sts.
Rnd 2:
Purl.
Rnd 3:
* P1, P2 tog; rep from * 5 (6, 7, 8) times more—12 (14, 16, 18) sts.
Rnd 4:
Purl. Do not change colors.
Rnd 5:
P2 tog 6 (7, 8, 9) times.
Cut yarn, leaving a 7" end. Draw end through rem sts and pull tight.

Thumb:
Divide 10 (12, 12, 14) sts from stitch holder onto 3 larger size double-pointed needles; with blue, pick up one st in thumb joining—11 (13, 13, 15) sts.
Continue in stripe pattern.
Rnd 1:
P9 (11, 11, 13), P2 tog.
Rnd 2:
Purl.
Rep Rnd 2 until thumb measures 1" (1 1/4", 1 1/2", 2") from joining. On last rnd, do not change colors.
Next Rnd:
P2 tog 5 (6, 6, 7) times.
Cut yarn, leaving a 7" end. Draw end through rem sts and pull tight. Weave in all ends.

Scarf
With straight needles and blue, cast on 39 (49) sts.
Edging:
Row 1 (right side):
Knit.

continued

Reverse Stripes (continued)

Row 2:
Purl.

Rows 3 through 6:
Rep Rows 1 and 2 twice more.

Row 7:
With off white, knit. Cut blue.

Ribbing:

Row 1 (wrong side):
K1; * P1, K1; rep from * across.

Row 2 (right side):
P1; * K1, P1; rep from * across.

Rep Rows 1 and 2 until ribbing measures 2" (2½"), ending by working a right side row.

Begin Stripe Pattern:

Note: Twist yarn on wrong side at end of rows. Carry unused colors along side edge. Slip markers as you come to them.

Row 1:
(K1, P1) 4 times; place marker; K23 (33), place marker; (P1, K1) 4 times.

Row 2:
With blue, (P1, K1) 4 times; P23 (33); (K1, P1) 4 times.

Row 3:
With blue, (K1, P1) 4 times; K23 (33); (P1, K1) 4 times.

Row 4:
With off white, (P1, K1) 4 times; P23 (33); (K1, P1) 4 times.

Row 5:
With off white, (K1, P1) 4 times; K23 (33); (P1, K1) 4 times.

Rep Rows 2 through 5 in sequence until scarf measures 40" (52") from ribbing, ending by working a Row 4. Cut blue.

Next Row:
With off white, knit.

Ending Ribbing:

Row 1 (right side):
P1; * K1, P1; rep from * across.

Row 2:
K1; * P1, K1; rep from * across.

Rep Rows 1 and 2 until ribbing measures 2" (2½"), ending by working a right side row. Join blue; cut off white.

EDGING

Row 1:
Knit.

Row 2:
Purl.

Rows 3 through 6:
Rep Rows 1 and 2 twice more.
Bind off.

Tie One On

Size:
Child Small

Finished Measurements:
Hat: 19" circumference
Mittens: 5" long
Scarf: 7" x 38"

Materials:

For Hat:
Worsted weight yarn, 1 oz (70 yds, 28 gms) pink; ½ oz (35 yds, 14 gms) lime

For Mittens:
Worsted weight yarn, 1 oz (70 yds, 28 gms) pink; ½ oz (35 yds, 14 gms) lime

For Scarf:
Worsted weight yarn, 8 oz (560 yds, 225 gms) pink; 1 oz (70 yds, 28 gms) lime

Note: Our models were made with Red Heart® Classic™, Grenadine #730 and Kiwi #651

Size 8 (5mm) 16" circular knitting needle, or size required for gauge (for hat, mittens and scarf)
Size 9 (5.5mm) double-pointed knitting needles (for cords, hat and mittens)
Stitch markers
Stitch holder (for mittens)
Size 16 tapestry needle

Gauge:
18 sts and 24 rows = 4" in stockinette st

Special Abbreviation

Slip, Slip, Knit (SSK):
Slip next 2 sts, one at a time, as to knit; insert left-hand needle through both sts from right to left; K2 tog—SSK made.

Instructions

Hat

Cord:
With lime and double-pointed needles, cast on 4 sts.
K4. Do not turn; * slide sts to other end of needle, bringing yarn across back of row, K4; rep from * until cord measures about 33" long. Cut yarn, draw end through 4 sts and pull tight.
Weave in ends.

Body:
Measure 7¾" from both ends of cord and mark with a safety pin or contrasting color thread.
With pink and circular needle, pick up 76 sts along edge of cord between marks. Turn.

Row 1 (wrong side):
K1, P74, K1.

Row 2 (right side):
K1; inc (knit in back and front of next st); K72, inc; K1—78 sts.

Row 3:
K1, P76, K1.

Row 4:
K1, inc; K74, inc; K1—80 sts.

Row 5:
K1, P78, K1.

Row 6:
K1, inc; K76, inc; K1—82 sts.

Row 7:
K1, P80, K1.

Row 8:
K1, inc; K78, inc; K1—84 sts.

Note: Remainder of hat is worked in rnds. Mark beg of each rnd.

Rnd 1:
Knit.
Rep Rnd 1 until hat measures 4" from beg.

Crown:
Rnd 1:
* K12, K2 tog; rep from * 5 times more—78 sts.

Rnd 2:
Knit.

Rnd 3:
* K11, K2 tog; rep from * 5 times more—72 sts.

Rnd 4:
Knit.

Rnd 5:
* K10, K2 tog; rep from * 5 times more—66 sts.

Rnd 6:
Knit.

Rnd 7:
* K9, K2 tog; rep from * 5 times more—60 sts.

Rnd 8:
Knit.

Rnd 9:
* K8, K2 tog; rep from * 5 times more—54 sts.

Rnd 10:
Knit.

Rnd 11:
* K7, K2 tog; rep from * 5 times more—48 sts.

Rnd 12:
Knit.

Rnd 13:
* K6, K2 tog; rep from * 5 times more—42 sts.

Rnd 14:
Knit.

Rnd 15:
* K5, K2 tog; rep from * 5 times more—36 sts.

Rnd 16:
* K4, K2 tog; rep from * 5 times more—30 sts.

Rnd 17:
* K3, K2 tog; rep from * 5 times more—24 sts.

Rnd 18:
* K2, K2 tog; rep from * 5 times more—18 sts.

Rnd 19:
* K1, K2 tog; rep from * 5 times more—12 sts.

Rnd 20:
* K2 tog six times—6 sts.

Cut yarn, draw end through rem sts and pull tight. Weave in all ends.

Top Knots
With lime and double-pointed needles, following cord instructions above, make 3 cords about 3" long.
Cut yarn, leaving a 6" end for sewing. Weave in beg end.
With 6" ends and tapestry needle, tack cords to top of hat.
Tie free end of each cord into a knot.

Mittens

Right Mitten:
With lime and double-pointed needles, make 12" cord following cord instructions. Measure 3" from each end; mark with a safety pin or contrasting thread.

continued

27

Tie One On (continued)

With pink and circular needle, pick up 26 sts along edge of cord between marks. Turn.

Row 1 (wrong side):
K1, P24, K1. Turn.

Row 2 (right side):
Knit. Turn.

Rows 3 and 4.
Rep Rows 1 and 2. At end of Rnd 4, do not turn.

Note: Remainder of mitten is worked in rnds; slip 9 sts onto one needle, slip 9 sts onto second needle, slip 8 sts onto third needle. Mark beg of each rnd.

Rnds 1 and 2:
Knit.

THUMB GUSSET:
Rnd 1:
K6; place marker; inc (knit in front and back of next st) twice; place marker; K18—28 sts.

Rnd 2:
Knit.

Rnd 3:
K6, inc; K2, inc; K18—30 sts.

Rnd 4:
Knit.

Rnd 5:
K6, inc; K4, inc; K18—32 sts.

Rnd 6:
Knit.

Rnd 7:
K6, inc; K6, inc; K18—34 sts.

Rnd 8:
Knit.

Rnd 9:
K6, inc; K8, inc; K18—36 sts.

DIVIDE FOR THUMB:
Rnd 1:
K18, place last 11 sts worked onto stitch holder; K18—25 sts. Remove markers.

Rnd 2:
K7, cast on 1 st (see **Figs 1** and **2**); K18—26 sts.

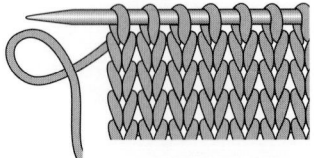

Fig 1

Fig 2

Rnd 3:
Knit.
Rep Rnd 3 until mitten measures 4½" from beg.

SHAPE TOP:
Rnd 1:
K3, K2 tog; K2, SSK (see Special Abbreviation on page 26); K7, K2 tog; K2, SSK; K4—22 sts.

Rnd 2:
Knit.

Rnd 3:
K2, K2 tog; K2, SSK; K5, K2 tog; K2, SSK; K3—18 sts.

Rnd 4:
Knit.

Rnd 5:
K1, K2 tog; K2, SSK; K3, K2 tog; K2, SSK; K2—14 sts.

Rnd 6:
Knit.

Rnd 7:
K2 tog; K2, SSK; K1, K2 tog; K2, SSK; K1—10 sts.

Rnd 8:
K2 tog five times—5 sts.
Cut yarn; draw end through rem sts and pull tight.

THUMB:
Divide 11 sts from stitch holder onto 3 double-pointed needles; pick up one st at thumb joining.

Rnd 1:
K10, K2 tog—11 sts.

Rnd 2:
Knit.
Rep Rnd 2 until thumb measures 1" from inside of thumb joining.

Next Rnd:
K2 tog five times; K1.
Cut yarn, draw end through rem sts and pull tight.
Tie cord ends into a square knot.

Left Mitten:
Work same as for Right Mitten to thumb gusset.

THUMB GUSSET:
Rnd 1:
K18, place marker, inc twice; place marker; K6—28 sts.

Rnd 2:
Knit.

Rnd 3:
K18, inc; K2, inc; K6—30 sts.

Rnd 4:
Knit.

Rnd 5:
K18, inc; K4, inc; K6—32 sts.

Rnd 6:
Knit.

Rnd 7:
K18, inc; K6, inc; K6—34 sts.

Rnd 8:
Knit.

Rnd 9:
K18, inc; K8, inc; K6—36 sts.

DIVIDE FOR THUMB:
Rnd 1:
K30, place last 11 sts worked onto stitch holder; K6—25 sts.

Rnd 2:
K19, cast on one st; K6—26 sts.

Rnd 3:
Knit.

Rep Rnd 3 until mitten measures 4½" from beg.

Shape Top:
Work same as for Right Mitten.

Thumb:
Work same as for Right Mitten.

Tie cord ends into a square knot.

Scarf

With lime and double-pointed needles, make cord 7" long following cord instructions on page 27.

With circular needle and pink, pick up 30 sts along edge of cord.

Row 1 (right side):
Knit.

Rep Row 1 until scarf measures 38" from beg, ending by working a right side row. With lime, cast on 4 sts (see **Figs 1** and **2**).

Bind off as follows:

Leaving sts on needle, * K3, SSK; sl 4 sts on right-hand needle back to left-hand needle; rep from * until no sts rem on left-hand needle. Cut yarn; draw ends through rem sts and pull tight.

Checked Out

Size:
Adult

Finished Measurements:
Hat: 22" circumference
Mittens: 7½" long with band

Materials:
For Hat:
Worsted weight yarn, 1½ oz (105 yds, 42 gms) each, black and white; 5 yds red
For Mittens:
Worsted weight yarn, 1½ oz (105 yds, 42 gms) each, black and white
Note: Our models were made with Lion Brand® Wool-Ease®, White #100, Black #153, and Ranch Red #102
Size 8 (5mm) 16" circular knitting needle, or size required for gauge (for hat)
Size 6 (4.25mm) 16" circular knitting needle (for hat)
Size 8 (5mm) double-pointed knitting needles, or size required for gauge (for hat and mittens)
Stitch markers
Stitch holder (for mittens)
Size 16 tapestry needle
Cotton balls or scraps of yarn (for stuffing top knot on hat)

Gauge:
With larger size needles:
20 sts and 28 rows = 4" in stockinette st

Special Abbreviation
Slip, Slip, Knit (SSK):
Slip next 2 sts, one at a time, as to knit; insert left-hand needle through both sts from right to left; K2 tog—SSK made.

Instructions
Note: Yarn not in use is carried loosely on wrong side of work. When changing colors, always bring new color under old color to prevent holes in work.

Hat
With smaller size circular needle and white, cast on 84 sts. Join, being careful not to twist sts.

Band:
Rnd 1:
Knit.
Rnd 2:
Purl.
Rnds 3 through 8:
Rep Rnds 1 and 2 three times more.
Change to larger size circular needle.

Body:
Rnd 1:
* With black, K1, with white, K2, (with black, K2, with white, K2) twice; with black, K1; place marker; rep from * 6 times more—7 sections of 12 sts each.
Note: On following rnds, sl section markers as you come to them. Mark beg of rnds.

Rnd 2:
With black, inc (knit in front and back of st) in next st; with white, K2, (with black, K2, with white, K2) twice; with black, inc; rep from * 6 times more—14 sts in each section.
Note: When knitting in the round, read every row on charts from right to left.

Rnds 3 through 15:
Work each section from **Chart A**.

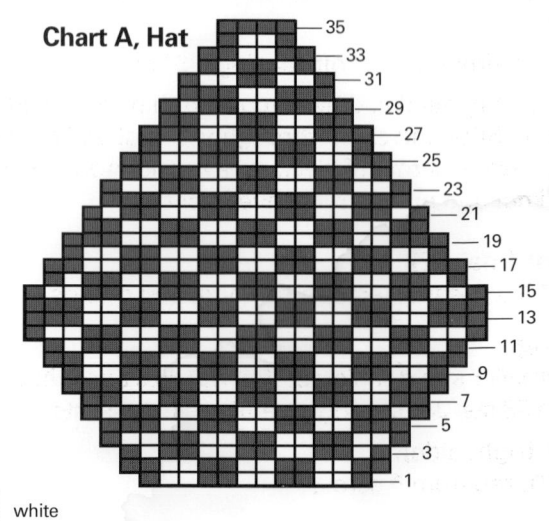

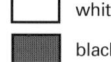

white
black

30

Decrease Rnds:
Note: Change to double-pointed needles when necessary.

Rnd 16:
Working color pattern from **Chart A**, K1, K2 tog; knit to 3 sts before next marker; SSK **(**see Special Abbreviation on page 30**)**; K1—22 sts in each section.

Rnds 17 through 35:
Continue working from **Chart A**, dec 2 sts in each section every other rnd. At end of Rnd 35—28 sts **(**4 sts in each section**)**. Cut white.

Top:
Note: Remove markers on next rnd.

Rnd 1:
Continuing with black, * K1, K2 tog; K1; rep from * around—21 sts.

Rnd 2:
* K5, K2 tog; rep from * around—18 sts.

Rnd 3:
* K2 tog; rep from * around—9 sts. Join red; cut black.

Top Knot:
Rnd 1:
* K1, inc; rep from * 3 times more; K1—13 sts.

Rnd 2:
Knit.

Rnd 3:
Inc in each st—26 sts.

Rnd 4:
* K2 tog; K1; rep from * 7 times more; K2—18 sts.

Stuff top knot with cotton or strands of yarn.

Rnd 5:
(K2 tog) 9 times. Finish off, leaving a 9" end.

With tapestry needle, draw end through rem sts and pull tight. Stick end down through top knot and out the bottom near last row of black; weave end around base of top knot and pull tight. Weave in end.

Mitten (make 2**)**
Note: Mitten is worked in rnds. Mark beg of rnds.

Ribbing:
With smaller size double-pointed needles and white, cast on 38 sts. Join, being careful not to twist sts.

Rnd 1 (right side**):**
* K1, P1; rep from * across.

Rep Rnd 1 until ribbing measures 2½".
Change to larger size double-pointed needles.

Body:
Note: When knitting in the round, read every row on charts from right to left.

Rnd 1:
With black, K3, with white, K2, (with black, K2, with white, K2) 3 times; with black, K4, with white, K2, (with black, K2, with white, K2) 3 times; with black, K3.

Rnds 2 through 6:
Work Rnds 2 through 6 of **Chart B**.

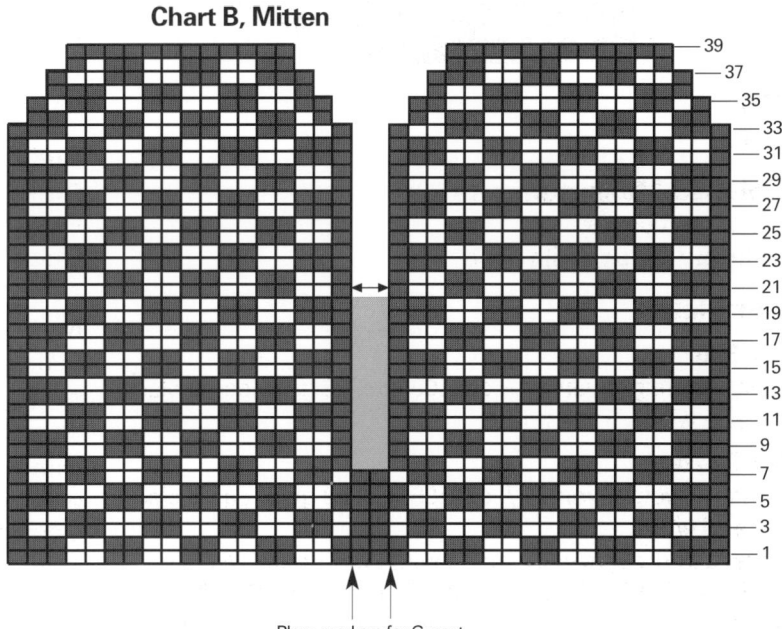

Chart B, Mitten

Place markers for Gusset

Rnd 7:
Continuing to work from **Chart B**, K18; place marker; K2; place marker; K18.

Rnd 8:
Referring to **Chart B**, knit to marker, slip marker; referring to **Gusset Chart**, * with black, K1 in front of next st, with white, K1 in back of same st—inc made; rep from * once more; slip marker; referring to **Chart B**, knit rem sts.

Gusset Chart

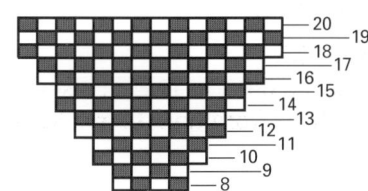

continued

31

Checked Out (continued)

Rnd 9:
Referring to **Chart B**, knit to first marker; slip marker; work from **Gusset Chart** to next marker; slip marker; working from **Chart B**, knit rem sts.

Rnds 10 through 19:
Work from **Chart B**, incorporating **Gusset Chart** between markers.

Rnd 20:
Working from **Chart B**, knit to first marker; remove marker; work gusset sts from **Gusset Chart**; slip gusset sts just worked onto stitch holder; remove second marker; working from **Chart B**, knit rem sts.

Hand:
Note: Chart B reflects open space. Center sts are now joined.

Rnds 21 through 33:
Work from **Chart B**, eliminating center sp.

Top:
Rnd 34:
Working from **Chart B**, * K1, K2 tog; K12; SSK (see Special Abbreviation on page 30); K1; rep from * once more.

Rnds 35 through 39:
Work from **Chart B**, dec as in prev rnd. At end of last rnd, cut white. Slip first 12 sts onto one needle; slip rem 12 sts onto 2nd needle. Referring to Special Technique on page 3, weave sts tog with black.

Thumb:
Divide 14 sts on stitch holder onto 3 double-pointed needles. With black, at end of 3rd needle, pick up 1 st in thumb joining.

Rnd 1:
Continuing in color pattern for gusset, knit to last 2 sts; K2 tog.

Rnd 2:
Knit.

Rep Rnd 2 until thumb measures 2½" from thumb joining. At end of last rnd, cut white.

Next Rnd:
With black, (K2 tog) 7 times. Cut yarn, leaving a 7" end. Draw end through rem sts and pull tight.

Weave in all ends.